MOTHER-DAUGHTER

POEMS

(and LETTERS)

MOTHER-DAUGHTER POEMS (and LETTERS)

Linda O'Dunn
&
Jordyn O'Dunn-Orto

The views and opinions expressed in this book are solely those of the author and do not reflect the views or opinions of Gatekeeper Press. Gatekeeper Press is not to be held responsible for and expressly disclaims responsibility of the content herein.

Mother-Daughter Poems (and Letters)

Published by Gatekeeper Press
2167 Stringtown Rd, Suite 109
Columbus, OH 43123-2989
www.GatekeeperPress.com

Copyright © 2020

by Linda O'Dunn and Jordyn O'Dunn-Orto

All rights reserved. Neither this book, nor any parts within it may be sold or reproduced in any form or by any electronic or mechanical means, including information storage and retrieval systems without permission in writing from the author. The only exception is by a reviewer, who may quote short excerpts in a review.

The cover design, interior formatting, and typesetting for this book are entirely the product of the author. Gatekeeper Press did not participate in and is not responsible for any aspect of these elements.

ISBN (paperback): 9781662904288

eISBN: 978166290429

DEDICATIONS

This book is dedicated to my daughters Alexandra, Charelle, and Jordyn, and to my mother Teresa (Oldham) Dunn. I would also like to dedicate it to the other strong women who have had an impact on my life – Vicky (my second mom), Minnie (of the James Bay Women's Group), and my cousins Beryl (whose strength and words inspire me) and Carole (our family historian and comedian).

Linda

This book is dedicated to my mother and my sisters, to the line of strong women from whom we descend, to the strong women we surround ourselves with, and to all the mothers and daughters around the world.

Jordyn

TABLE OF CONTENTS

Jordyn Stephanie Jean 1

Thirteen 2

Jordyn 4

Mother 5

Daughter Of Mine 6

Fighting 7

I Have A Mother 8

I Have A Daughter 9

My Mother 10

A Diamonte For My Daughters 11

A Poem For 2010 12

My Saviour 14

A Mother's Love 15

A Daughter's Love 17

Things My Mother Taught Me 20

Last Child Standing 24

Eighteen 30

Empty Nest 33

A Limerick For The Lights Of My Life 34
My Mother's Embrace 35
My Daughter's Hands 37
University Graduate 38
Author bios 44

Jordyn Stephanie Jean

What can I write for you, daughter number three,
To let you know how very much you mean to me?

I thought I had held my last baby in my arms,
But here you are, captivating me with your charms.

People ask "Are you disappointed? Did you hope
    for a son?"
How foolish, I am not disappointed in you, little one!

What a shaky start we had, my lovely girl,
As we laboured to bring you into this world,

And the ordeal wasn't over once you were born,
In the end I lay curled in a ball, in agony and worn.

It was your father who held you and bonded with
    you,
My turn would come later, alone, just we two.

And now, my darling, as I hold you to my breast and
    you smile up at me
I thank God for the gift of you, my beautiful
    daughter number three!

August 22, 1993

THIRTEEN

August 22, 2006

My darling Jordyn,

You are thirteen years old today! It doesn't seem that long ago that I held you in my arms. You have been so anxious to grow up, my daughter number three. Well, today you take one giant step toward that goal. You are no longer a child. But remember, sweetheart, you are not an adult yet either.

You have looked forward to becoming a teenager and you have some wonderful, exciting years ahead of you, during which you will grow from a young girl to a young woman. But these years can also be hard ones, baby, as you deal with the pressures of your peers, boys, drugs, alcohol, and other difficult issues. It is an "in-between" time - between childhood and adulthood - where you don't fit completely in either world, where you're trying to figure out who you are, and what you want to do with your life.

I look forward to this next stage of your life with excitement, Jordyn, but also with a little sadness. In just five short years my baby — my last born — will leave the nest. I want those years to be great ones for us, sweetheart, so remember what I told you only a short while ago. I am not the enemy! I have the same goal you do – for you to grow up. I want you to become a strong, independent woman who makes her own decisions.

That transition is a process, honey, it isn't instantaneous. Please be patient just a little longer. Allow this to happen gradually.

I know from experience that we will survive your teenage years, and I know we will be friends, my beautiful daughter number three. I so look forward to that. In the meantime, I'm still raising you. I'm not your friend yet. I'm your mother. It is my job – still – to teach you right from wrong, to have you face the consequences of mistakes and bad choices, to motivate you to want to be the best that you can be.

You have been through a lot in your thirteen years, baby. You have dealt with the divorce of your parents, the loss of your beloved dog, Rebel, the awful day you were bitten, and your two older sisters flying the nest – going off on their own adventures and leaving you behind. You have shown courage and perseverance through all of this, Jordyn. I have faith in you, sweetheart. I know you will make good choices and be true to yourself. I know you will grow up, in these next five years, to be an honest, responsible, compassionate young woman – a woman I will be as proud of as I am of the young girl you are now.

I love you, Sweetheart,
Mom
xoxoxoxoxoxoxoxoxo

Joyful

One of a Kind

Radical

Daring

Youthful

Never Gives Up

MY GIRL!

MOTHER

Marvellous

Over-protective

Teacher

Helpful

Ethical

Right

I LOVE MY MOTHER !!

DAUGHTER OF MINE

Dear to my heart
Always a part of me
Unusual, untidy, unforgettable
Gracious, grateful, giving
Hugs me when I'm feeling low
Teaches me to be young again
Embraces life – with arms wide open!
Remember always who you are-a beautiful young
   woman, and who you come from - a
   long line of strong women.

FIGHTING

I hate it when we fight,
You are my shining light,
You make everything seem right.

Sometimes I don't want to talk to you,
Sometimes I need my own space too,
But that is about me, babe, not you.

I'm only human; I get angry, make mistakes,
But when the moment has passed, and I'm calm again,
I just want to hold you close - I hate causing you pain.

I know sometimes I push you away,
I don't always know the right thing to say,
But your smile is the brightest thing in my day.

I love you – UNCONDITIONALLY
mom
xoxo

I HAVE A MOTHER

I have a mother.
I'm not her first or only,
But she treats me like no other.

She laughs with me,
And she plays with me.
She shows me what is right.

She treats me like a lady,
Though I act like such a child.

She may yell at me.
She may cry at me.
She may laugh at me.

One thing remains the same.
She will always laugh **with** me.
She will always cry **with** me.
And she will always yell **with** me.

She is my mother.

December 17, 2008

I HAVE A DAUGHTER

I have a daughter, she's not my first or only,
But without her my life would be so lonely.

She's my daughter number three,
She's my Jordyn Stephanie Jean.

She has her own special beauty and her gran's blue eyes,
She is loving, smart, compassionate, and wise.

She makes me laugh, she makes me cry,
She gives me hope, she shows me why.

She forgives my faults and temper, shows me how to make a new start.
Her smile brightens my day, her laughter warms my heart.

I wouldn't want to live in a world without my daughter number three,
Her smiles, her laughter, her hugs, and love mean everything to me.

MY MOTHER

My, isn't she wonderful?
You're jealous she is mine.

Mothering is her forté
On everything, she is right!
There isn't a time she's not there
Holding me so dear
Everybody loves her
Right now and forever, I love her most!

A DIAMONTE FOR MY DAUGHTERS

DAUGHTERS
BEAUTIFUL, BODACIOUS
GIGGLING, GABBING, GLADDENING
FEARLESSNESS, FRAGILITY, FERVENCY, FAITH
LABOURING, LOVING, LIBERATING
PRIVILEGED, PROUD
MOTHER

A POEM FOR 2010

Jordyn, my girl, I know you've had a bad year.
My heart has hurt watching you shed bitter tears.

A friend you loved as a sister let you down.
But you didn't let that turn your life around.

You had to face the sorrow of a friend taking her
    own life,
While dealing with school and all of life's normal
    strife.

Backing off, watching you learn from your mistakes
    was hard to do,
But sometimes, my girl, that was the best way that I
    could help you.

It's been a year of liking boys who didn't like you,
And being unable to date the ones who do,
Of staying true to yourself – how proud I am of you!

I told you one day that you had let me down.
I wish I could take back those words, the hurt, your
    frown.

Let me go back and do it over – tell you what I really
   meant to say;
It was normal teenage behavior that drove me to rant
   that day,
But you, my darling girl, have never let me down in
   any way!

MY SAVIOUR

When my shoulders get too heavy with the burdens that I bear,
You put your arms around me and tell me to let you share.

When the tears run down my face, and all I can do is cry,
You hold me to your chest and tell how proud you are I tried.

And when my worries and my doubts take a hold of me,
You look me in the eye and help me see what you see.

My mother, you are amazing – this is very true.
If I'm half as good as you, then I'll be awesome too!

Mother, I love you, and I know that you will always love me too.

June 09, 2010

A MOTHER'S LOVE

My family means the world to me. I was raised to never take for granted my loved ones. So I have always cherished my family, and striven to form strong bonds with them. In the tragedy of my friend's suicide, they became my strength, the people I leaned on the most, and our bonds grew. But with my father and sisters several provinces away, it was my mother's arms that I turned to the most.

I have always loved my mother, and likewise always felt the love she has for me. The proof of her love can be seen in every aspect of my life; the poems written by her that decorate my bedroom walls, in the room she forfeited for me, the school maps she sat and colored with me, the clothes I wear that she bought for me instead of for herself. Throughout my childhood, my parents' divorce, and the several moves we made after the divorce, her love has been constant. When a dog bite deformed part of my face, and I was teased and bullied, mom was there. Her support for math, theatre, sports, writing, and self-growth has never wavered. Even through our arguments and fights – which, no matter the strength of the bond, a mother and her teenage daughter will face – she has cared for me. I am her Bella Mia, loved around the world and back again, to infinity and beyond; I am her daughter number three.

So it may be clear that I have never doubted my mother's love for me, but never have I been more thankful for her than I was during that time. I truly believe that I would not have made it through without my mother. The gratitude I feel for her cannot be put into words. It was her arms I turned to when I heard the news, her shoulder I cried on, her hand I clutched, and her voice that became my beacon. The safety and comfort she provided were unequaled and unparalleled.

I do not know if she understands this; if she is aware that by holding my hand, she also held my life together. And so I would like to say to my mother: "You not only had the power to bring me into this world, you have the power to keep me in it. I love you."

A DAUGHTER'S LOVE

My family means the world to me. I was raised by parents who loved, encouraged and supported me. Because both my parents and my older sister died young, and I felt their loss so deeply, I tried to raise my daughters to never take their family for granted. I tried to teach them that friends, and even lovers and husbands, may come and go in their lives, but that their family would always be there for them. I know from bitter experience that when you lose a parent or a sibling there is no one in this world who understands exactly what you are going through like a brother or a sister. Some people will breeze through life for many years before death reaches out its ugly hand to touch their lives; others will learn too early the agony of loss. You, my daughter number three, were not lucky in this; you learned at sixteen that you were not immortal or untouchable. But you also learned, my darling girl, the power, the strength of family as you turned to yours to support you through that difficult time.

I have always loved my daughters, with a

strength and fierceness that I cannot describe. Most mothers feel this primal, protective love for their children; not all are blessed, honoured, to be told so clearly and with such passion that their love is recognized and returned. The proof of **your** love, my girl, is in the poems you have written for me (that I cherish more than diamonds and gold), in your willingness to accept my help with your school work, in your seeing and appreciating that sometimes I did without things so that you could have them (just as my mother once sacrificed her needs and desires for mine). It is in your forgiving me for breaking up your happy home when you were only six, it is in your forgiving my mistakes and the arguments and fights that were so hard on both of us. It has been my honour to support you through the hard times in your life, and my joy to watch your triumphs. I always felt such love and pride as I watched you run down the basketball court, strut down the catwalk, command the audience's attention on the stage. There is one thing in this life upon which you can always count, my love will be constant - and unconditional.

It is clear that you have never doubted my love

for you. I am thankful that I could be there for you during that time, my love. The gratitude you feel **has** been put into words - meaningful, beautiful words that have touched my heart deeply. My arms were made to hold you, my shoulder molded for your head to rest upon, my hand always open to receive yours, and my voice - I did not know it had such power, until you called it your beacon. I wish with all my heart that I could have shielded you from that experience, that pain. I wish that I could always shield you from life's storms, but I know the best that I can do is to be your safe harbour and comfort during those storms.

    I did not understand until reading your letter how close you were to drowning in your sadness and despair. I thank you with all my heart, Jordyn Stephanie Jean, for not giving into that darkness, for allowing me to help you find the strength to wait for it to lift, to show you the love and light that are still in this world. My hand is always here, my daughter number three, to hold you to this life, because I could not live my life if you were not in it. I love you, Bella Mia, around the world and back again, to infinity and beyond!

THINGS MY MOTHER TAUGHT ME

My momma raised me right.

Said strength isn't found at the bottom of a bottle and courage isn't just a pretty word, it's a way of life.

Taught me my dragons may not have scales, evil witches won't have warts, knights don't come in shining armor, and I can't rely on a genie to grant my wishes.

Told me that I can't sleep forever, walking in the woods alone isn't safe, you can't climb hair, and no man is called Charming.

Showed me that my weapons won't be a shield and sword, no flaming arrows will fly from my bow, and I need to stop idolizing the heroines in my books because I really have no idea how to use a sword, and I rely on my fists in a fight.

So I may not ride off on a snow white stallion into an amber setting sun as beams of gold light up my hair, but that's okay because I never did take horseback riding lessons, and I prefer chestnut mares anyway.

My momma raised me right.

Said she's been there, seen the damage that resulted in hollowed cheeks and sunken eyes, and never wanted her daughter number three going down that road.

Made sure that I never relied on any vices to get me through the day or spent my nights huddled on a lonely city's abandoned sidewalks.

Ensured I wasn't the kind to go running when life got too hard, wouldn't submerge my fears in tequila or blaze away my problems while writing lyrics that start with 'getting together and feeling all right.'

Had me promise that cigarettes wouldn't be resting on puffed, cracked lips, previously used needles wouldn't pierce prominently blue veins, and crayola coloured tablets wouldn't dissolve on my tongue into rave lit, love drug butterflies.

So I won't be the girl holding out her cap or climbing into men's beds, sucking down on detrimental toxins to push away the pain, and hell, I don't even eat that much chocolate.

My momma raised me right.

Said I'm a proud, independent woman, no one

rules my life but me, my choices are my own, and damn it I'm strong enough to take on the world.

Helped me realize that it isn't the days I spent in bathroom stalls graffiti-ed with my name, crying till my throat was sore that holds purchase on my soul; it's the day I stood and walked away.

Swore to me that even though I ran then, when it mattered I stayed and fought because being good, being just, and being kind matter to me.

Embodied in me a belief system that had me straightening my back, and running from nothing – but spiders!

Taught me that confidence isn't built from putting others down, and self esteem is looking in the mirror, picking out every flaw that I have and leaving the house without make-up on anyway.

Showed me that beauty doesn't come from high fashion labels, expensive grooming, or a number on a scale. It is in the sparkle in my eyes, the smile on my lips, the outbursts of giggles, my messy buns and thin-rimmed glasses.

Praised me for being a young woman who can look at a world where bombs go off faster than text messages, government bills deny gay rights, teenagers laugh at a girl who is not afraid to dance alone – and still say that life is amazing.

So maybe Disney didn't write the story of my life, but I know my life won't be ending in an article on the effects of addiction and abuse, with a girl who hides her dreams behind her hair, or a woman who walks in the world afraid to really live.

Because my momma raised me right. And I love her for it.

LAST CHILD STANDING

Child of my Change of Life

Born two months before my thirty fifth birthday, you were the child of my early onset menopause. Hot flashes, mood swings, anxiety, depression. The turbulent, ever-changing weather of my hormones set the climate of your childhood. I had less energy and patience to give to you than I had for your sisters who were born when I was in my twenties. What I seemed to have more of at that stage of my life – and which I know drove you crazy – was fear. That fear was all pervasive; it affected every decision I made involving you, at times it overwhelmed me. I wasn't afraid to let you go; I trusted you, I believed in you. I was afraid to lose you – to accident, to evil design, to the fickleness of the gods, to the fate that awaits those whose mothers fail to remain ever vigilant. I was afraid for your sisters too, but I know you felt the yoke of my over protectiveness even more than they did.

Child of my Grief

Born just five months before the too early death of my mother, you were the child of my grief and anger. Whether they remember the difference or not, your older sisters had six and nine years of being raised by a relatively happy mother. For the decade following mom's death I was an angry, wounded woman.

There were periods of time when I managed to suppress that pain and anger; at other times it was more obvious, more raw. The fact remains that the rage and torment were always there, eating away at me, tainting every aspect of my life, including my parenting. I grieve for the fact that my youngest child didn't know the me I was before the death of my mother.

Child of Divorce

All three of my daughters, immersed in three very different stages of development when we separated, struggled to deal with the divorce of their parents; all three of them suffered. You, however, my daughter number three, had to make choices your older sisters didn't have to. When you were not quite eleven years old you made an agonizing decision; to leave my home to go to live with your father. I understood completely that you had made this choice because you felt that you needed to have more time than summer and Christmas visits allowed to get to know your dad. Three years later you made another painful decision; to come back to live with me. You were a young teenage girl who recognized that you needed the presence and guidance of your mother as you grew to womanhood. Despite the fact that your father and I tried to let you know we respected and supported you, and were not hurt by your decisions, you were inevitably haunted by the feeling that you were choosing one parent over another, hurting the parent whose home you had decided to leave. It broke my heart, my child, that you found yourself in such an untenable situation. These are choices no child should ever have to make.

Child of my Despair

Unhappy, unfulfilled, unconnected for so long, how could I have been the parent I truly wanted to be to you? There were times during the last few years you lived at home when I felt that I was barely keeping my head above water. I fought desperately to hold onto hope and not slip into the deep, dark depression I felt lapping at my heels. Somehow I managed to keep clinging to the belief that my life was going to get better. I tried so hard not to let my despair impact you, Jordyn, but I know it did. I saw the confusion in your eyes when I reacted so strongly to something we both knew was so insignificant. That look hurt me, it haunted me; it made me want to crawl away and die. For so many years I pushed my pain, anger, fear and unhappiness away. I told myself to just hang on, I was almost finished raising you – "Don't let the volcano erupt, don't spoil this time, don't hurt your child." Some days, baby, that was too hard and I failed. I was living with physical pain, mental anguish, emotional burnout, and spiritual emptiness. I am so sorry, my baby, that I took out my frustrations on you. You helped me realize that I had to dig deeper for the strength I needed. I had to find patience, rediscover gratitude, and remember the joy being a mother – being your mother – gave me.

Child of my Reflection

I felt for a long time, my darling, that there was a volcano building inside me. I was afraid to let it explode, so I managed to keep the lid on most of the time, but there have always been eruptions – sometimes small ones, sometimes huge ones. The lava of my emotions, however, was never fully released; it was always there, boiling beneath the surface. Working on my book was cathartic, but it was also very difficult. Memories and emotions that had been buried for years rose to the surface. The eruptions were more frequent and more intense. Unfortunately, Jordyn, you were the child who was present, witnessing and being affected by, that long overdue rite of passage. Thank you for your patience with me and for forgiving those outbursts. In writing those stories and reading (and re-reading, and re-reading!) them I was reliving all those experiences. But I was also reflecting, learning, and growing. I was crying, raging, and letting go. I truly believed there was an end in sight – an easing of pain and anger too long ignored. I took a leave of absence from a job that was crippling me physically, mentally and emotionally. I tried hard to find a better release for my emotions than volcanic eruptions. I promised myself that I would begin each day again with gratitude, hope, and inspiration. I started again.

Child of Mine

Oh, beautiful child of mine! You are also the child of my hope, the child of my inspiration, my saving grace. You are the last babe to be held in my arms, the last tyrannical toddler, the last charming child, the last precocious preteen, the last tenacious teenager. I hope that I have shown you more than erratic hormonal behavior, grief, despair, and desperation. I pray that I have also shown you my joy, passion, gratitude and hope. How colourless, stale, and empty those last years would have been without you in them. What would I do without you in my life, beautiful child of mine?

I love you more than life itself! Around the world and back again!
Mom
xoxo

EIGHTEEN

July 11, 2011

Dear Jordyn,

I can't believe I am finished raising my last child!

I am happy.

There is a sense of completion - of finishing a very
   important job.
There is a sense of gratitude - for all the love and
   happiness you have given me.
There is a sense of pride - as I look at the amazing young
   woman you have become.

But I am also sad.

That my parenting journey is ending.
That my last child has grown up and is leaving the nest.
That I won't hear your bubbly voice and see your smiling
   face every morning.

I am going to miss you, darling.

There are still so many things I want to teach you and
   share with you.

Where did the time go? Where has the little girl I used to
   hold in my arms gone?
You have faced so much already in your young life,
Jordyn, and you have learned many things about yourself.
You have suffered pain, loss, teasing, and rejection, but
you didn't let those things define you. You are defined by
your loving heart, your inner strength, and your courage.
You are not beaten and belittled; you are bold, brave, and
bodacious.

Thank you, daughter number three, for coming back to live
with me. Thank you for the privilege of watching you grow
to womanhood. Thank you for the honour of being your
mom full time again.

What an amazing journey it has been watching you grow
from a tiny, helpless infant to the strong, confident,
beautiful young woman you are today. I have watched
your face shine with joy, crumple with defeat, and twist with
grief. I have watched you run, stumble, fall, and get back
up again.

You are an incredible young woman, Jordyn. You have such courage, idealism, and passion. I don't know what the future holds for you, hon, but I am confident that you can handle whatever life throws your way.

Stay strong, have courage, believe in yourself, follow your heart, and always know that I love you - around the world and back again!

EMPTY NEST

Wait - don't go - I'm not ready!
I didn't say all the words I meant to say, teach all the lessons I meant to teach.
I haven't taught you how to cook all your favourite recipes.
I forgot to show you how to iron and how to hem your jeans.
You aren't even eighteen years old yet.
You can't begin to imagine all the things that might go horribly wrong - but I can.
You shouldn't ever be afraid to try, to fail, or to come home.
Please don't ever be cavalier about your safety; don't trust that handsome stranger, walk down that dark alley alone, leave your drink unattended.
But wait - just one more kiss!
Wait - just one more hug!
Wait - just one more glimpse of your beautiful face before you turn and walk away!
Wait,
Wait,
Oh no - it happened too fast - again!

Written July, 2011 after dropping Jordyn off at Victoria Airport

A LIMERICK FOR THE LIGHTS OF MY LIFE

In my younger days I was wild and free.
Then I settled down and had daughters - three.
My hair's gone grey from its brown.
What was once up has gone down.
Now life after kids is all about me!

MY MOTHER'S EMBRACE

My Mother's Thumbs

My mother's thumbs are aged, with creases like silk and polished nails. When I am scared, they mold flawlessly into her fists. When I am sad, their delicate pads brush away my tears. And when my mother holds me, her absent-minded thumbs caress the back of my hand, soothing worries I do not yet have.

My mother's thumbs are perfect.

My Mother's Hands

My mother's hands are wrinkled with age and marked by the sun. They are both delicate and powerful, able to soothe and throw a punch. Her hands are perpetually outstretched; to coax me into my first steps, to swing me high into the air, to dance with me, and catch me when I fall. I have always reached for my mother's hands.

My mother's hands are perfect.

My Mother's Arms

My mother's arms are tan, marked, and dotted with freckles. They are soft, molding themselves around my frame, yet the muscles underneath are poised to protect and defend. They are infinitely long, capable of wrapping me up a thousand times over. My mother's arms do not waver or shake; they are steadfast.

My mother's arms are perfect.

My Mother's Shoulders

My mother's shoulders are smooth and supple. They are sturdy; strong enough to bear the weight of the world and protect her daughters from all evils. They are feather light, dancing as her body shakes with laughter. I cling to my mother's shoulders, they are my sanctuary.

My mother's shoulders are perfect.

My mother's embrace is flawless. It is safe and reliable, constant and cherished. It is home.

My mother's embrace is perfect.

MY DAUGHTER'S HANDS

Tiny and wrinkled, they wrapped around my finger,
    relying on my strength.
Little and hurting, they reached for mommy's hand,
    relying on my care.
Small and trusting, they tightly clasped my hand,
    relying on my love.
Larger and stronger, they pulled away from me,
    relying on themselves.
Big as mine, we work side by side,
    relying on each other.
Strong and steady, they reach to give me support,
    now I rely on her.

UNIVERSITY GRADUATE

I have so many things to say to you I don't know
   where to start.
I know I want to make clear to you the pride that fills
   my heart.

I wonder if you realize how very much you have
   achieved.
In just 23 years you've done more than I could have
   foreseen.

You have overcome so many things, my girl, in your
   short life.
I have watched as you struggled with hardships and
   with strife.

You attended six schools in three cities and one
   small town.
But always being new kid on the block couldn't keep
   you down.

One of the worst days of your life must have been
   the day that you were bitten.

How my mother's heart wishes that chapter had
    never been written.

You took being bullied, for that and other things, in
    your stride.
You carry that small scar with honour, it is your
    badge of pride.

You had to make hard choices that no child should
    have to make.
Living with your mother or your father - so afraid to
    cause heartache.

One of the hardest things I've ever done is letting
    you walk away.
You coming back for your high school years meant
    more than words could ever say.

Distance, disinterest, and death caused the
    shedding of many tears
As you dealt with the heavy loss of friendship during
    your teenage years.

I've always told you that character isn't built on an
    easy life.

You've built your character, my darling, dealing with those hardships and strife.

Thankfully, your life has been filled with good challenges, too.
You learned to be part of a team, and found the leader within you.

I loved watching you race down the basketball court, giving it your all.
Win or lose, you were such a good sport, in my eyes you always stood tall.

Improv was so much fun; I was always so proud seeing you perform on stage.
I didn't have the courage to do anything like that when I was your age.

You held fast to your convictions, didn't give into the pressure of your peers.
I know it was sometimes hard to stand alone, to make your boundaries clear.

You made friends who shared your triumphs and stood by when things were bad.

When I see the bond that still exists between you, it
    makes my heart feel glad.

Your first hero was Blueberry Bert, as a young girl
    Disney princesses were your choice.
But by the time you were a teen, you were wise
    enough to speak with your own voice.

We shared so much, my Bella Mia, during your high
    school years.
There was closeness and fighting, songs and poems,
    laughter and tears.

We threw rocks and sticks to ease our anger at
    Esquimalt Lagoon.
Ate ice-cream at Saxepoint, took long walks
    beneath full moons.

You left for a gap year of travel and exploration at
    just eighteen years old.
You worked hard to earn your way, taking on a
    nurturing, mother's role.
Your experiences and adventures have led to the
    forming of a very wise soul.

These four years you've been at university have
 absolutely flown.
With so many miles between us, you know you have
 truly done this on your own.
There have been some bumps and hurdles, but I'm
 so proud of how much you've grown.

You had two older sisters to follow, and that wasn't
 an easy task.
But you have found your own way, Jordyn, and you
 walk your own path.

You live your life with passion, you have a mighty
 heart.
This year is not an ending; it is a brand new start.

I so love our summer reunions in our city by the sea.
Enjoying bacon-wrapped scallops, sangria, and
 peach Bellini's.

Strolls through Dragon and Fan Tan Alleys,
 noodles and bubble tea.
At least one visit to Esquimalt Lagoon for a walk
 beside the sea.

A highlight of each summer is our road trip in my small car.
Always singing, laughing, talking, just being who we are.

You fill me with awe, Jordyn Stephanie Jean, I am so very proud of you.
I will always admire your strength, courage, loyalty, compassion, and world view.

You have grown up hearing of the long line of strong women from whom you descend.
You can proudly join that line my girl; I knew that's how this poem would end.

AUTHOR BIOS

JORDYN O'DUNN-ORTO loves reading and writing poetry, travelling, and spending time with her family and friends. She graduated from Esquimalt High in Victoria and attended the University of Winnipeg, where she earned a bachelor's degree in conflict resolution. Jordyn has always been passionate about equality and the importance of being kind to one another. She lives in Winnipeg, Canada and works as a career counsellor at a high school. She is also training with an Alberta based company to present workshops on bully prevention to students, teachers, and parents.

LINDA O'DUNN is passionate about teaching, writing, and travelling. As the daughter of a military bandsman, she led a nomadic life, living in Germany for several years and in various towns across Canada, from the east to west coasts. Linda also graduated from Esquimalt High in Victoria and attended the University of Winnipeg, where she earned a bachelor's degree in education. As an adult, Linda continued to move around Canada, also lived in England, and recently spent six years teaching English in Saudi Arabia. Linda currently lives and teaches in Abbotsford, Canada, but she considers Victoria to be her home, and that is where she plans to eventually settle down.

www.ingramcontent.com/pod-product-compliance
Lightning Source LLC
LaVergne TN
LVHW011859060526
838200LV00054B/4433